CONTENTS

Chapter 1
The Basics of Cognitive-Behavioral Therapy (CBT)

Anxiety is a common mental health condition that affects millions of people worldwide. It is characterized by persistent feelings of worry, fear, and apprehension that can interfere with daily life. Anxiety disorders include generalized anxiety disorder (GAD), panic disorder, social anxiety disorder, and specific phobias, among others. Understanding anxiety is the first step in managing it effectively.

Cognitive-Behavioral Therapy (CBT) is a widely recognized and effective treatment for anxiety. CBT focuses on identifying and changing negative thought patterns and behaviors that contribute to anxiety. By addressing these underlying issues, individuals can develop healthier ways of thinking and coping with anxiety.

History and Development of CBT CBT was developed in the 1960s by Dr. Aaron T. Beck, a psychiatrist who noticed that his patients with depression often had negative thoughts that influenced their emotions and behaviors. Dr. Beck's work led to the development of cognitive therapy, which later evolved into cognitive-behavioral therapy as behavioral techniques were integrated. The integration of cognitive and behavioral approaches created a powerful method for addressing mental health issues, including anxiety.

CBT is based on several core principles:

- Cognitive Principle: Thoughts influence emotions and behaviors. By changing negative thought patterns, individuals can improve their emotional and behavioral responses.

- Behavioral Principle: Behaviors are learned and can be unlearned. By modifying behaviors, individuals can reduce anxiety and improve their quality of life.

- Collaborative Principle: CBT is a collaborative process between the therapist and the individual. It involves setting goals, working together to achieve them, and monitoring progress.

- Structured and Time-Limited: CBT is typically structured and time-limited, focusing on specific problems and goals. Sessions often follow a structured format, with homework assignments to reinforce learning.

- Goal-Oriented and Problem-Focused: CBT focuses on specific problems and goals. This makes it practical and relevant to the individual's everyday life.

- Empirical Principle: CBT relies on evidence-based techniques that have been proven effective through scientific research.

CBT helps individuals with anxiety through several key mechanisms:

- Identifying Negative Thoughts: Recognizing and understanding negative thought patterns that contribute to anxiety. This involves becoming aware of automatic thoughts and cognitive distortions, such as catastrophizing or overgeneralization.

- Challenging Negative Thoughts: Learning to challenge and reframe these negative thoughts to reduce their impact. This process, known as cognitive restructuring, involves evaluating the evidence for and against a thought and developing more balanced and realistic perspectives.

- Behavioral Techniques: Implementing behavioral techniques such as exposure therapy to confront and reduce anxiety triggers. Exposure therapy involves gradually facing feared situations in a controlled manner to reduce avoidance and build confidence.

- Developing Coping Skills: Equipping individuals with practical coping skills to manage anxiety in everyday life. This includes relaxation techniques, problem-solving skills, and assertiveness training.

Components of CBT for Anxiety

- Cognitive Restructuring: Cognitive restructuring involves identifying and challenging irrational or maladaptive thoughts. For example, a person who believes "I will fail at everything I try" learns to evaluate this belief critically and replace it with a more balanced thought like "I have succeeded in many things before, and I can learn from my mistakes."

- Behavioral Experiments: These are activities designed to test the validity of negative beliefs. For instance, someone with social anxiety might conduct an experiment where they engage in a conversation and observe the outcome, challenging their belief that others will always judge them negatively.

- Exposure Therapy: This involves gradually exposing individuals to feared situations or objects to reduce their anxiety response. Over time, repeated exposure helps individuals learn that the feared outcomes are unlikely and that they can cope with anxiety.

- Relaxation Techniques: CBT often includes training in relaxation techniques such as deep breathing, progressive muscle relaxation, and mindfulness meditation. These techniques help manage physical symptoms of anxiety.

- Activity Scheduling and Behavioral Activation: Encouraging individuals to engage in positive and rewarding activities can help reduce feelings of anxiety and improve mood. Structured scheduling of activities can provide a sense of accomplishment and pleasure.

- Problem-Solving Skills: Teaching individuals effective problem-solving skills can empower them to tackle challenges that contribute to anxiety. This involves identifying problems, generating possible solutions, evaluating and choosing the best solution, and implementing it.

Benefits of CBT for Anxiety CBT offers several benefits for individuals with anxiety:

- Evidence-Based: Numerous studies have demonstrated the effectiveness of CBT for various anxiety disorders. It is considered the gold standard treatment for anxiety.

- Empowering: CBT empowers individuals by teaching them skills to manage their anxiety independently. This fosters a sense of control and self-efficacy.

- Long-Lasting Effects: The skills learned in CBT can provide long-lasting relief from anxiety. Many individuals continue to use CBT techniques long after therapy has ended.

- Flexible: CBT can be adapted to suit individual needs and preferences. It can be conducted in individual, group, or online formats.

Real-Life Example:

Consider the case of Sarah, a 30-year-old woman with social anxiety disorder. Sarah feared social interactions and often avoided parties, meetings, and even casual conversations. In CBT, Sarah worked with her therapist to identify her negative thoughts, such as "People will think I'm boring" and "I'll say something stupid." Through cognitive restructuring, she learned to challenge these thoughts and replace them with more balanced ones, like "Some people might not be interested in what I say, but others will be" and "Everyone makes mistakes in conversations." She also engaged in exposure therapy by gradually attending social events and practicing her coping skills. Over time, Sarah's anxiety decreased, and she felt more confident in social situations.

Chapter 2
Identifying and Challenging Negative Thoughts

Negative thoughts play a significant role in perpetuating anxiety. Cognitive-Behavioral Therapy (CBT) emphasizes the importance of recognizing and challenging these thoughts to manage anxiety effectively. This chapter will delve into the process of identifying negative thoughts, understanding cognitive distortions, and implementing strategies to challenge and replace them with healthier, more realistic thoughts.

Cognitive distortions are irrational thought patterns that can contribute to anxiety and other emotional issues. These distortions often occur automatically and can distort reality in a way that reinforces negative thinking. Common cognitive distortions include:

- All-or-Nothing Thinking: Viewing situations in black-and-white terms without recognizing any middle ground. For example, thinking, "If I don't succeed at this task, I am a complete failure."

- Overgeneralization: Making broad conclusions based on a single event. For example, believing, "I made a mistake in my presentation; I'm always terrible at public speaking."

- Catastrophizing: Expecting the worst possible outcome in any situation. For example, fearing, "If I make a mistake, everyone will think I'm incompetent, and I'll lose my job."

- Mental Filtering: Focusing solely on the negative aspects of a situation while ignoring the positive. For example, dwelling on a minor criticism while disregarding praise.

- Disqualifying the Positive: Rejecting positive experiences by insisting they don't count for some reason. For example, thinking, "They only said nice things to be polite, not because I did a good job."

- Jumping to Conclusions: Making negative assumptions without evidence. This includes mind reading (assuming others are thinking negatively about you) and fortune telling (predicting negative outcomes).

- Emotional Reasoning: Assuming that negative emotions reflect the truth. For example, thinking, "I feel anxious, so there must be something wrong."

- Should Statements: Using "should" or "must" statements to impose unrealistic expectations on oneself or others. For example, "I should always be calm and composed."

- Labeling and Mislabeling: Attaching a negative label to oneself or others based on a single incident. For example, calling oneself a "loser" after one setback.

- Personalization: Taking responsibility for events outside of one's control. For example, believing, "It's my fault that the meeting didn't go well."

The first step in challenging negative thoughts is to become aware of them. This process involves self-monitoring and reflection. Here are some techniques to help identify negative thoughts:

- Thought Records: Keeping a daily journal to record situations that trigger anxiety, the thoughts that arise in response, and the emotions and behaviors that follow. This helps individuals track patterns in their thinking.

- Mindfulness Practices: Practicing mindfulness can increase awareness of automatic thoughts and help individuals observe them without judgment.

- Reflection Questions: Asking questions such as "What was going through my mind just before I started feeling anxious?" or "What am I afraid might happen?" can uncover underlying negative thoughts.

Once negative thoughts are identified, the next step is to challenge and reframe them. This process involves several techniques:

- Socratic Questioning: This involves asking oneself a series of questions to challenge the validity of negative thoughts. Examples include:
    - What evidence do I have for and against this thought?
    - Are there alternative explanations?
    - What would I say to a friend who had this thought?
    - How likely is it that my fear will come true?
    - What is the worst that could happen, and how could I cope with it?

- Cognitive Restructuring: This involves replacing negative thoughts with more balanced and realistic ones. For example, changing "I will fail at everything" to "I may struggle with some things, but I have succeeded in many others."

- Evidence Collection: Gathering evidence that contradicts negative thoughts can help challenge them. For instance, listing past achievements can counteract the thought "I can't do anything right."

- Behavioral Experiments: Conducting experiments to test the validity of negative thoughts. For example, if someone fears they will embarrass themselves in a social situation, they can gradually expose themselves to such situations and observe the outcomes.

- Thought Stopping: Using techniques to interrupt negative thoughts, such as saying "Stop!" to oneself or visualizing a stop sign, followed by redirecting attention to a positive or neutral thought.

Case Study: Overcoming Catastrophizing

Consider John, a 35-year-old man with generalized anxiety disorder. John often catastrophized about his work performance, believing that any mistake would lead to his dismissal. Through CBT, John learned to identify this cognitive distortion and challenge it using Socratic questioning. He asked himself, "What evidence do I have that I will be fired for a mistake?" and realized that he had received positive feedback from his supervisors. He also conducted a behavioral experiment by volunteering for a challenging project and successfully completing it, which further disproved his catastrophic thinking.

Case Study: Managing Social Anxiety

Emma, a 28-year-old woman with social anxiety disorder, often believed that others were constantly judging her negatively. Her automatic thoughts included "People will think I'm boring" and "I'll embarrass myself." Through CBT, Emma kept a thought record and used Socratic questioning to challenge these thoughts. She asked herself, "What evidence do I have that people find me boring?" and "Have I embarrassed myself in social situations before?" She found that people often enjoyed her company and that she had not made any significant social blunders. Emma also practiced exposure therapy by gradually attending social events, which helped her build confidence and reduce her anxiety.

Chapter 3
Behavioral Activation

Behavioral Activation (BA) is a crucial component of Cognitive-Behavioral Therapy (CBT) that focuses on changing behaviors to improve mood and reduce anxiety. This chapter will explore the principles of behavioral activation, how it works, and practical strategies for implementing it in daily life. By understanding and applying BA techniques, individuals can break the cycle of avoidance and inactivity that often exacerbates anxiety.

Behavioral Activation is based on the idea that changing behavior can lead to changes in mood. It targets the avoidance patterns that are common in anxiety disorders. Avoidance may provide short-term relief from anxiety but often leads to long-term negative consequences, such as increased isolation, decreased activity levels, and worsening anxiety.

The Role of Avoidance in Anxiety Avoidance behaviors are actions taken to escape or prevent anxiety-provoking situations. While avoidance can temporarily reduce anxiety, it often reinforces the belief that the situation is dangerous or unmanageable, which can increase anxiety over time. Examples of avoidance behaviors include:

- Social Withdrawal: Avoiding social situations to prevent feelings of embarrassment or judgment.

- Procrastination: Putting off tasks that cause anxiety, such as work assignments or household chores.

- Safety Behaviors: Relying on specific actions or objects to feel safe, such as carrying a water bottle to avoid dry mouth during a presentation.

Principles of Behavioral Activation Behavioral Activation involves several key principles:

- Activity Monitoring: Tracking daily activities to identify patterns of avoidance and inactivity.

- Activity Scheduling: Planning and engaging in activities that are likely to improve mood and reduce anxiety.

- Gradual Exposure: Facing avoided situations in a controlled and gradual manner to reduce fear and build confidence.

- Positive Reinforcement: Increasing engagement in activities that provide a sense of accomplishment and pleasure.

- Problem-Solving: Addressing obstacles that prevent engagement in positive activities.

How Behavioral Activation Works Behavioral Activation works by:

- Increasing Activity Levels: Engaging in meaningful and enjoyable activities can improve mood and provide a sense of accomplishment.

- Breaking the Cycle of Avoidance: Confronting avoided situations helps reduce anxiety and build confidence.

- Enhancing Social Connections: Participating in social activities can reduce feelings of isolation and provide social support

- Improving Problem-Solving Skills: Developing effective problem-solving skills can help individuals overcome barriers to activity engagement.

Implementing Behavioral Activation involves several steps:

- Activity Monitoring: Begin by keeping a record of daily activities and rating mood levels throughout the day. This helps identify patterns of avoidance and inactivity.

- Identifying Values and Goals: Reflect on personal values and long-term goals. Consider activities that align with these values and goals, as they are more likely to be meaningful and motivating.

- Activity Scheduling: Plan specific activities to engage in each day. Start with small, manageable tasks and gradually increase the difficulty and frequency of activities.

- Gradual Exposure: Identify avoided situations and create a hierarchy of feared activities, ranging from least to most anxiety-provoking. Gradually face these situations, starting with the least anxiety-provoking and working up to more challenging ones.

- Positive Reinforcement: Reward yourself for completing activities, especially those that were challenging. This can be through self-praise, small treats, or engaging in a favorite activity.

- Problem-Solving: Identify and address obstacles that may prevent engagement in planned activities. Develop strategies to overcome these obstacles.

Detailed Steps for Activity Scheduling

- Set Specific Goals: Break down larger goals into smaller, more manageable tasks. For example, if the goal is to "increase physical activity," a smaller task might be "go for a 10-minute walk three times a week."

- Prioritize Activities: Identify which activities are most important or most likely to improve mood and schedule those first.

- Balance Pleasurable and Necessary Activities: Ensure a mix of activities that provide pleasure and those that are necessary for daily functioning. For example, balance fun hobbies with essential chores.

- Use a Planner or Calendar: Write down scheduled activities in a planner or calendar to provide structure and accountability.

- Start Small: Begin with activities that are easy to accomplish to build momentum and confidence. Gradually increase the complexity and duration of activities.

Case Study: Overcoming Social Anxiety through Behavioral Activation

Consider Emily, a 27-year-old woman with social anxiety disorder. Emily avoided social gatherings and interactions at work, leading to increased feelings of isolation and anxiety. Through Behavioral Activation, Emily began by monitoring her daily activities and identifying patterns of avoidance. She then set a goal to increase her social interactions. Emily created a hierarchy of social situations, starting with small tasks like greeting coworkers and gradually working up to attending a team meeting. By gradually exposing herself to these situations and rewarding herself for her efforts, Emily was able to reduce her social anxiety and build confidence in her social skills.

Detailed Case Study: Managing Generalized Anxiety with Behavioral Activation Michael, a 45-year-old man with generalized anxiety disorder, experienced significant anxiety related to work and home responsibilities. He often procrastinated on important tasks, leading to increased stress and feelings of overwhelm. Through Behavioral Activation, Michael started by keeping an activity log to monitor his daily routines. He identified that his avoidance behaviors were contributing to his anxiety. Michael set specific goals, such as "complete one work report each day" and "spend 30 minutes organizing the garage." He scheduled these tasks in his calendar and used positive reinforcement by treating himself to a favorite snack or a short break after completing tasks. Over time, Michael found that his anxiety decreased as he became more proactive and engaged in his daily activities.

Chapter 4
Exposure Therapy

Exposure Therapy is a fundamental component of Cognitive-Behavioral Therapy (CBT) that involves confronting fears to reduce anxiety. By systematically and gradually exposing individuals to anxiety-provoking situations, Exposure Therapy helps reduce avoidance behaviors and build confidence. This chapter will explore the principles of Exposure Therapy, how it works, and practical strategies for implementing it in daily life.

Exposure Therapy is based on the principle that facing feared situations can help reduce the anxiety associated with them. The goal is to break the cycle of avoidance and fear by gradually confronting these situations in a controlled and safe manner. Over time, this leads to habituation, where the anxiety response diminishes, and individuals learn that they can handle the feared situation without catastrophic outcomes.

Exposure Therapy can be conducted in several ways, including:

- In Vivo Exposure: Directly confronting feared objects, situations, or activities in real life. For example, someone with social anxiety might attend a social event.

- Imaginal Exposure: Vividly imagining the feared situation when direct exposure is not possible. This is often used for traumatic memories or fears that are difficult to encounter in real life.

- Interoceptive Exposure: Confronting physical sensations that are feared. This is particularly useful for panic disorder, where individuals might fear the physical sensations of anxiety, such as a racing heart.

- Virtual Reality Exposure: Using virtual reality technology to simulate feared situations. This can be useful for fears that are difficult to recreate in real life, such as flying.

The process of Exposure Therapy involves several steps:

- Assessment: Identifying the specific fears and avoidance behaviors that contribute to anxiety. This includes understanding the triggers, intensity, and frequency of anxiety.

- Creating an Exposure Hierarchy: Developing a list of feared situations, ranked from least to most anxiety-provoking. This helps structure the exposure process and ensures a gradual approach.

- Developing a Plan: Planning the exposure sessions, including the duration, frequency, and specific activities. The plan should be realistic and tailored to the individual's needs.

- Conducting Exposure Sessions: Gradually exposing the individual to feared situations, starting with the least anxiety-provoking and moving up the hierarchy. The focus is on facing the fear without engaging in avoidance or safety behaviors.

- Processing and Reflection: Reflecting on the experience after each exposure session, discussing what was learned, and reinforcing the progress made.

An exposure hierarchy is a graded list of feared situations that helps guide the exposure process. Here is an example for someone with social anxiety:

- Saying hello to a neighbor.

- Making a small purchase at a store and chatting briefly with the cashier.

- Asking a stranger for directions.

- Attending a small social gathering with friends.

- Introducing oneself to a new group of people.

- Giving a short presentation at work or in a class.

- Attending a large social event with unfamiliar people.

- Speaking in front of a large audience.

During exposure sessions, it is essential to follow these guidelines:

- Stay in the Situation: Remain in the feared situation until the anxiety decreases significantly. This helps demonstrate that the feared outcomes are unlikely and that anxiety will naturally decrease over time.

- Avoid Avoidance Behaviors: Refrain from behaviors that provide temporary relief from anxiety but reinforce fear in the long term. For example, avoiding eye contact during a conversation.

- Practice Regularly: Conduct exposure sessions regularly to reinforce learning and build confidence. Consistency is key to the success of Exposure Therapy.

- Use Relaxation Techniques: Practice relaxation techniques, such as deep breathing or mindfulness, before and after exposure sessions to manage anxiety levels.

Case Study: Overcoming Fear of Flying

Consider Sarah, a 34-year-old woman with a severe fear of flying. Her fear was so intense that she avoided all air travel, limiting her ability to visit family and pursue career opportunities. Through Exposure Therapy, Sarah worked with her therapist to create an exposure hierarchy:

- Watching videos of planes taking off and landing.

- Visiting an airport and observing planes from a distance.

- Sitting in a stationary plane on the ground.

- Taking a short, simulated flight using virtual reality.

- Booking a short domestic flight and sitting on the plane with the door open.

- Taking a short domestic flight with the door closed but remaining on the ground.

- Taking a short, real flight with a trusted friend.

Sarah began by watching videos of planes, gradually working up the hierarchy. Over several months, she faced each step, using relaxation techniques to manage her anxiety. Eventually, Sarah was able to take a short flight, significantly reducing her fear of flying and expanding her travel opportunities.

Case Study: Confronting Social Anxiety through Exposure

Emily, a 28-year-old woman with social anxiety disorder, found it challenging to speak up in meetings at work. Her exposure hierarchy included steps like:

- Making a comment in a one-on-one conversation with a trusted colleague.

- Asking a question during a small team meeting.

- Giving a short presentation in front of a small group of coworkers.

- Leading a team meeting for a brief segment.

- Presenting a full report during a department-wide meeting.

Emily began with the least anxiety-provoking step and gradually worked her way up the hierarchy. With each step, she practiced relaxation techniques beforehand and reflected on her experiences afterward. Over time, Emily's confidence grew, and her anxiety in social situations decreased significantly.

Chapter 5
Developing Coping Skills

Coping skills are essential tools for managing anxiety and improving overall well-being. These skills help individuals navigate challenging situations, reduce stress, and maintain emotional balance. This chapter will explore a variety of coping strategies, including relaxation techniques, problem-solving skills, and lifestyle changes, that can help individuals manage anxiety effectively.

Coping skills are crucial for several reasons:

- Reducing Anxiety: Effective coping strategies can help lower anxiety levels and prevent escalation.

- Improving Resilience: Coping skills enhance resilience, enabling individuals to bounce back from stressful situations more quickly.

- Enhancing Emotional Regulation: These skills help manage and regulate emotions, leading to better mental health.

- Promoting Well-being: Coping strategies contribute to overall well-being and improve the quality of life.

Coping skills can be categorized into several types, each with its unique benefits:

1. Relaxation Techniques
2. Cognitive Strategies
3. Behavioral Strategies
4. Problem-Solving Skills
5. Lifestyle Changes

Relaxation techniques help reduce physical and emotional tension, promoting a state of calm and relaxation. Here are some effective relaxation techniques:

- Deep Breathing: Deep breathing exercises involve taking slow, deep breaths to calm the nervous system. This technique can be practiced anywhere and helps reduce immediate anxiety.

- Exercise: Simple Deep Breathing
    - Sit comfortably with your back straight.
    - Inhale slowly through your nose, counting to four.
    - Hold your breath for a count of four.
    - Exhale slowly through your mouth, counting to six.
    - Repeat for several minutes, focusing on the rhythm of your breath.

- Progressive Muscle Relaxation (PMR): PMR involves tensing and then relaxing different muscle groups in the body, promoting overall relaxation.

- Exercise: Progressive Muscle Relaxation
    - Find a quiet place where you won't be disturbed.
    - Sit or lie down comfortably.
    - Starting with your toes, tense the muscles as tightly as you can for about five seconds.
    - Relax the muscles completely and focus on the tension leaving your body.
    - Move up through your body, tensing and relaxing each muscle group.

- Guided Imagery: This technique involves visualizing calming and peaceful scenes to reduce anxiety and promote relaxation.

- Exercise: Guided Imagery
  - Sit or lie down in a comfortable position.
  - Close your eyes and take a few deep breaths.
  - Imagine yourself in a serene and peaceful place, like a beach or a forest.
  - Focus on the details of this place: the sounds, smells, and sights.
  - Spend several minutes visualizing this scene, allowing yourself to feel calm and relaxed.

- Mindfulness Meditation: Mindfulness involves focusing on the present moment without judgment. Regular mindfulness practice can reduce anxiety and improve emotional regulation.

- Exercise: Mindfulness Meditation
  - Find a quiet place to sit comfortably.
  - Close your eyes and take a few deep breaths.
  - Focus on your breath, noticing the sensation of the air entering and leaving your body.
  - When your mind wanders, gently bring your focus back to your breath.
  - Continue for 10-15 minutes, practicing non-judgmental awareness of the present moment.

- Yoga and Tai Chi: These mind-body practices combine physical movement with deep breathing and meditation, promoting relaxation and reducing anxiety.

- Exercise: Simple Yoga Sequence
  - Begin with a few minutes of deep breathing to center yourself.
  - Practice a series of gentle yoga poses, such as child's pose, cat-cow, and downward dog.
  - Focus on your breath and the sensations in your body as you move through the poses.
  - End with a few minutes of deep relaxation in savasana (corpse pose).

Cognitive strategies involve changing the way individuals think about and interpret situations. These strategies help reframe negative thoughts and reduce anxiety:

- Cognitive Restructuring: This technique involves identifying and challenging negative thoughts, replacing them with more balanced and realistic ones.

- Exercise: Cognitive Restructuring Worksheet
    - Identify a negative thought and write it down.
    - Challenge the thought by asking for evidence for and against it.
    - Replace the negative thought with a more balanced and realistic one.
    - Reflect on how this new thought makes you feel.

- Positive Self-Talk: Encouraging oneself with positive affirmations and supportive statements can counteract negative thinking.

- Exercise: Positive Self-Talk Practice
    - Write down a list of positive affirmations that resonate with you.
    - Each morning, read the list out loud to yourself.
    - Repeat the affirmations throughout the day, especially when you notice negative thoughts.

- Thought Stopping: Interrupting negative thought patterns by saying "stop" and redirecting attention to positive or neutral thoughts.

- Exercise: Thought Stopping Technique
    - When you notice a negative thought, say "stop" out loud or in your mind.
    - Immediately redirect your attention to a positive thought or a neutral activity.
    - Practice this technique consistently to break the habit of negative thinking.

- Visualization: Visualizing successful outcomes or positive experiences can reduce anxiety and build confidence.

- Exercise: Positive Visualization
    - Find a quiet place to sit comfortably.
    - Close your eyes and take a few deep breaths.
    - Visualize a situation where you feel anxious, but imagine yourself handling it confidently and successfully.
    - Focus on the positive emotions and sensations associated with this successful outcome.
    -

Behavioral strategies involve changing actions and behaviors to reduce anxiety. These strategies help individuals engage in positive activities and reduce avoidance behaviors:

- Activity Scheduling: Planning and engaging in enjoyable and meaningful activities can improve mood and reduce anxiety.

- Exercise: Activity Scheduling Planner
    - List activities that you enjoy and find meaningful.
    - Schedule at least one of these activities into your daily routine.
    - Reflect on how engaging in these activities impacts your mood and anxiety levels.

- Exercise: Regular physical activity releases endorphins, reduces stress, and improves overall mental health.

- Exercise: Creating an Exercise Routine
    - Choose a physical activity that you enjoy, such as walking, running, or dancing.
    - Set a goal to engage in this activity for at least 30 minutes, three to five times a week.
    - Track your progress and notice the positive effects on your mood and anxiety.

- Exposure Therapy: Gradually confronting feared situations to reduce anxiety and build confidence.

- Exercise: Exposure Hierarchy
    - Identify situations that cause you anxiety and rank them from least to most anxiety-provoking.
    - Start with the least anxiety-provoking situation and gradually work your way up the hierarchy.
    - Reflect on your progress and celebrate your successes along the way.

- Social Support: Seeking support from friends, family, or support groups can provide emotional comfort and reduce feelings of isolation.

- Exercise: Building a Support Network
    - Identify people in your life who are supportive and understanding.
    - Schedule regular check-ins or social activities with these individuals.
    - Consider joining a support group to connect with others who share similar experiences.

Problem-Solving Skills Problem-solving skills help individuals address and resolve challenges that contribute to anxiety. Effective problem-solving involves several steps:

- Identify the Problem: Clearly define the problem and its impact on your life.

- Generate Possible Solutions: Brainstorm a list of potential solutions without judging their feasibility.

- Evaluate and Select Solutions: Assess the pros and cons of each solution and choose the most effective one.

- Implement the Solution: Put the chosen solution into action and monitor its effectiveness.

- Reflect and Adjust: Reflect on the outcome and make any necessary adjustments to improve the solution.

- Exercise: Problem-Solving Worksheet
    - Define a problem you are facing.
    - Brainstorm possible solutions and evaluate each one.
    - Select and implement the best solution, then reflect on the outcome.
    - Adjust the solution as needed and repeat the process for new challenges.

Certain lifestyle changes can significantly reduce anxiety and improve overall well-being. Here are some beneficial lifestyle changes:

- Healthy Diet: Eating a balanced diet rich in fruits, vegetables, lean proteins, and whole grains can improve mood and reduce anxiety.

- Exercise: Nutrition Plan
    - Create a weekly meal plan that includes a variety of healthy foods.
    - Incorporate foods known to reduce anxiety, such as leafy greens, nuts, and fatty fish.
    - Track your eating habits and notice any changes in your mood and anxiety levels.

- Sleep Hygiene: Prioritizing good sleep hygiene by maintaining a regular sleep schedule and creating a relaxing bedtime routine.

- Exercise: Sleep Hygiene Checklist
    - Set a consistent bedtime and wake-up time.
    - Create a bedtime routine that includes calming activities, such as reading or taking a warm bath.
    - Avoid caffeine, alcohol, and electronics before bed.

- Limiting Caffeine and Alcohol: Reducing the intake of caffeine and alcohol, which can exacerbate anxiety.

- Exercise: Caffeine and Alcohol Log
  - Track your consumption of caffeine and alcohol for one week.
  - Identify patterns and situations where you consume these substances.
  - Set goals to reduce or eliminate caffeine and alcohol from your diet.

- Time Management: Effectively managing time to reduce stress and create a balanced schedule.

- Exercise: Time Management Planner
  - List your daily and weekly tasks and prioritize them.
  - Create a schedule that includes time for work, self-care, and leisure activities.
  - Reflect on how effective time management impacts your stress and anxiety levels.

- Hobbies and Interests: Engaging in hobbies and activities that bring joy and fulfillment.

- Exercise: Hobbies and Interests List
  - Make a list of hobbies and activities that you enjoy.
  - Schedule regular time for these activities in your routine.
  - Reflect on how engaging in hobbies impacts your mood and anxiety.

Case Study: Implementing Coping Skills

Consider Jack, a 40-year-old man with generalized anxiety disorder. Jack often felt overwhelmed by work responsibilities and personal commitments. By working with a therapist, Jack learned to implement various coping skills:

- Relaxation Techniques: Jack practiced deep breathing and mindfulness meditation daily to reduce his immediate anxiety.

- Cognitive Strategies: He used cognitive restructuring to challenge and replace negative thoughts about his work performance.

- Behavioral Strategies: Jack scheduled regular exercise and engaged in hobbies like gardening to improve his mood.

- Problem-Solving Skills: He used problem-solving techniques to address work-related challenges, such as delegating tasks and setting realistic deadlines.

- Lifestyle Changes: Jack improved his diet, prioritized sleep, and reduced caffeine intake, which significantly reduced his overall anxiety levels.

Chapter 6
Mindfulness and CBT

Mindfulness is the practice of paying attention to the present moment with an open, non-judgmental attitude. When integrated with Cognitive-Behavioral Therapy (CBT), mindfulness enhances the ability to manage anxiety by increasing awareness of thoughts and emotions, and by promoting acceptance and self-compassion. This chapter will explore the principles of mindfulness, how it complements CBT, and practical strategies for integrating mindfulness into anxiety management.

Mindfulness is rooted in ancient meditation practices but has been adapted into modern therapeutic approaches. It involves consciously bringing attention to the present moment and accepting it without trying to change or avoid it. The practice of mindfulness can help individuals:

- Increase Self-Awareness: Mindfulness helps individuals become more aware of their thoughts, feelings, and bodily sensations, leading to greater self-understanding.

- Reduce Reactivity: By observing thoughts and emotions without immediate reaction, mindfulness helps reduce impulsive responses to anxiety triggers.

- Enhance Emotional Regulation: Mindfulness promotes a balanced emotional response, reducing the intensity of negative emotions and enhancing positive ones.

- Promote Acceptance: Mindfulness encourages acceptance of thoughts and feelings as they are, without judgment or resistance.

Mindfulness complements CBT by addressing the way individuals relate to their thoughts and emotions. While CBT focuses on identifying and challenging negative thoughts, mindfulness encourages observing those thoughts without judgment. The integration of mindfulness into CBT, often referred to as Mindfulness-Based Cognitive Therapy (MBCT), has been shown to be particularly effective in managing anxiety and preventing relapse.

Mindfulness-Based Cognitive Therapy (MBCT) combines traditional CBT techniques with mindfulness practices to help individuals manage anxiety. Key components include:

- Mindful Awareness: Developing the ability to observe thoughts, emotions, and physical sensations without getting caught up in them. This awareness helps individuals recognize patterns of negative thinking and avoid automatic responses.

- Decentering: Learning to see thoughts as mental events rather than as facts. This shift in perspective reduces the power of negative thoughts and allows for a more objective view of experiences.

- Acceptance: Cultivating an attitude of acceptance towards all experiences, whether positive or negative. Acceptance does not mean resignation but rather an openness to experiencing thoughts and emotions without trying to change or avoid them.

- Self-Compassion: Practicing kindness and understanding towards oneself, especially in moments of difficulty. Self-compassion helps counteract the harsh self-criticism often associated with anxiety.

Integrating mindfulness into daily life can significantly enhance the effectiveness of CBT. Here are some mindfulness practices that can help manage anxiety:

- Mindful Breathing
  - Exercise: Sit comfortably with your eyes closed. Focus on your breath as it flows in and out of your body. Notice the sensation of the breath entering through your nose, filling your lungs, and then leaving your body. If your mind wanders, gently bring your focus back to your breath. Practice this for 5-10 minutes daily.

- Body Scan Meditation
  - Exercise: Lie down in a comfortable position and close your eyes. Begin by focusing on your toes, noticing any sensations. Gradually move your attention up through your body—feet, legs, abdomen, chest, arms, hands, neck, and head. As you focus on each part of your body, observe any sensations without trying to change them. This practice can be particularly helpful in releasing physical tension associated with anxiety.

- Mindful Observation
  - Exercise: Choose an object in your environment, such as a flower or a cup. Spend a few minutes observing it closely. Notice its color, texture, shape, and any other details. This practice helps cultivate focus and brings attention to the present moment, reducing anxiety about past or future concerns.

- Mindful Walking
  - Exercise: Take a walk at a slow, deliberate pace. Focus on the sensation of your feet touching the ground, the movement of your legs, and the rhythm of your breath. Notice the sights, sounds, and smells around you. Mindful walking is a powerful way to bring mindfulness into everyday activities.

- Loving-Kindness Meditation
  - Exercise: Sit comfortably with your eyes closed. Begin by focusing on your breath. Then, silently repeat phrases such as "May I be happy, may I be healthy, may I be at peace." After a few minutes, extend these wishes to others, including loved ones, acquaintances, and even those with whom you have conflicts. This practice fosters self-compassion and reduces anxiety related to interpersonal relationships.

Mindfulness can be integrated into CBT in various ways to enhance anxiety management:

- Mindful Awareness in Cognitive Restructuring
  - Before challenging a negative thought, practice mindful awareness by observing the thought without judgment. Notice the emotions and physical sensations that accompany the thought. This practice helps create a space between the thought and your reaction, allowing for more effective cognitive restructuring.

- Mindfulness in Exposure Therapy
  - During exposure sessions, use mindfulness to stay present with the anxiety-provoking situation. Focus on your breath and bodily sensations as you face the feared situation. Mindfulness helps reduce the urge to avoid or escape and allows you to experience the situation fully, leading to habituation.

- Mindful Acceptance of Emotions
  - When you experience intense emotions, such as fear or sadness, practice mindful acceptance. Acknowledge the emotion without trying to change it. Notice where it is felt in your body and observe it with curiosity. This practice reduces the intensity of emotions and promotes emotional regulation.

- Mindful Breaks During the Day
  - Incorporate short mindfulness practices into your daily routine. For example, take a few moments to focus on your breath before starting a meeting or practice mindful observation during a meal. These mindful breaks help reduce stress and keep you grounded throughout the day.

Case Study: Integrating Mindfulness into CBT

Consider Emily, a 35-year-old woman with social anxiety disorder. Emily often found herself ruminating on negative thoughts about her interactions with others, leading to heightened anxiety. Her therapist introduced her to MBCT, combining traditional CBT techniques with mindfulness practices.

- Mindful Awareness: Emily began practicing mindful breathing daily, which helped her become more aware of her anxious thoughts without getting caught up in them. This awareness allowed her to identify and challenge cognitive distortions more effectively.

- Decentering: By practicing mindfulness, Emily learned to see her thoughts as just thoughts, not facts. This shift in perspective reduced the power of her negative thoughts and helped her approach social situations with less fear.

- Acceptance: Emily practiced mindful acceptance of her anxiety, recognizing that it was a natural response rather than something to be avoided. This acceptance reduced her fear of anxiety itself, making it easier for her to engage in exposure therapy.

- Self-Compassion: Through loving-kindness meditation, Emily developed greater self-compassion, which helped her overcome the harsh self-criticism that often accompanied her social anxiety. As a result, she became more confident and resilient in social situations.

The Science Behind Mindfulness and CBT Numerous studies have demonstrated the effectiveness of combining mindfulness with CBT for anxiety management. Research shows that mindfulness practices can:

- Reduce Anxiety Symptoms: Mindfulness has been shown to decrease the severity of anxiety symptoms by helping individuals disengage from negative thought patterns.

- Improve Emotional Regulation: Mindfulness strengthens the brain's ability to regulate emotions, particularly in areas such as the prefrontal cortex, which is responsible for decision-making and impulse control.

- Enhance Cognitive Flexibility: Mindfulness promotes cognitive flexibility, allowing individuals to shift their perspective and approach problems from different angles.

- Prevent Relapse: MBCT has been particularly effective in preventing relapse in individuals with recurrent depression and anxiety, as it teaches them to recognize early signs of distress and respond skillfully.

Mindfulness and Neuroplasticity One of the most compelling aspects of mindfulness is its impact on neuroplasticity—the brain's ability to change and adapt. Regular mindfulness practice has been shown to:

- Increase Grey Matter Density: Studies have found that mindfulness meditation can increase grey matter density in brain regions associated with learning, memory, and emotional regulation.

- Strengthen Connectivity: Mindfulness enhances connectivity between different brain regions, particularly those involved in attention and self-regulation.

- Reduce Amygdala Activity: The amygdala, a brain region involved in the fear response, shows reduced activity in individuals who practice mindfulness regularly. This reduction is associated with decreased reactivity to stress and anxiety.

Mindfulness in Everyday Life Integrating mindfulness into everyday activities can help sustain its benefits beyond formal meditation sessions. Here are some ways to incorporate mindfulness into daily life:

- Mindful Eating
    - Practice mindful eating by paying full attention to the experience of eating. Notice the colors, textures, and flavors of your food. Eat slowly, savoring each bite, and observe how your body feels as you eat. Mindful eating can reduce stress, prevent overeating, and enhance your relationship with food.

- Mindful Communication
    - Engage in mindful communication by being fully present during conversations. Listen attentively without planning your response or interrupting. Notice the tone, body language, and emotions of the person you are speaking with. Mindful communication fosters deeper connections and reduces misunderstandings.

- Mindful Work
    - Bring mindfulness to your work by focusing on one task at a time. Avoid multitasking, and take breaks to reset your focus. Notice how you feel physically and mentally during the workday, and practice mindful breathing or stretching to reduce stress.

- Mindful Driving
    - Practice mindfulness while driving by paying attention to the sensations of driving, the environment around you, and your emotional state. Notice the feel of the steering wheel, the sound of the engine, and the movement of the car. Mindful driving can reduce road rage and increase safety.

Mindfulness can enhance relationships by promoting empathy, understanding, and emotional regulation. Here are some ways mindfulness can improve relationships:

- Active Listening: Mindful listening involves fully focusing on the speaker without distraction. This practice shows respect and fosters a deeper connection.

- Emotional Awareness: Mindfulness helps individuals become more aware of their emotions, allowing them to communicate more effectively and respond rather than react in conflicts.

- Compassion and Empathy: Mindfulness cultivates compassion and empathy by encouraging individuals to see things from others' perspectives and respond with kindness.

Self-compassion is a crucial aspect of mindfulness that involves treating oneself with the same kindness and understanding as one would offer to a friend. Self-compassion has been shown to reduce anxiety and depression and increase resilience. Here's how to cultivate self-compassion:

- Mindful Self-Compassion Exercise:
  - Sit comfortably and close your eyes. Place a hand over your heart and take a few deep breaths. Silently repeat phrases such as "May I be kind to myself" or "May I accept myself as I am." Focus on the feelings of warmth and care you direct toward yourself.

- Handling Self-Criticism:
  - When you notice self-critical thoughts, pause and take a mindful breath. Acknowledge the thought without judgment and respond with a self-compassionate statement, such as "It's okay to make mistakes" or "I'm doing my best."

- Self-Compassion Break:
  - When you're feeling stressed or overwhelmed, take a self-compassion break. Pause and acknowledge your feelings, remind yourself that everyone struggles at times, and offer yourself kindness and understanding.

Chapter 7
Cognitive Restructuring

Cognitive restructuring is a core component of Cognitive-Behavioral Therapy (CBT) that involves identifying and challenging negative thought patterns and replacing them with more balanced and realistic thoughts. This chapter will delve into the principles of cognitive restructuring, provide detailed techniques for challenging cognitive distortions, and offer practical strategies for applying these techniques to manage anxiety effectively.

Cognitive restructuring is based on the idea that our thoughts, emotions, and behaviors are interconnected. Negative thoughts can lead to negative emotions and unhelpful behaviors, which can reinforce the cycle of anxiety. By challenging and changing these negative thoughts, cognitive restructuring helps break this cycle and promotes healthier emotional responses.

The cognitive triangle is a fundamental concept in CBT that illustrates the relationship between thoughts, emotions, and behaviors:

- Thoughts: What we think about a situation influences how we feel and act. For example, the thought "I'm going to fail" can lead to feelings of anxiety and avoidance behaviors.

- Emotions: Our emotions are directly linked to our thoughts. Negative thoughts often lead to negative emotions, such as fear, sadness, or anger.

- Behaviors: How we act in response to our thoughts and emotions can either reinforce or reduce those thoughts and feelings. Avoidance, for example, can reinforce anxiety.

Cognitive restructuring focuses on changing the "thought" aspect of the triangle to create more positive emotions and behaviors.

Cognitive distortions are irrational or exaggerated thought patterns that can contribute to anxiety. Recognizing these distortions is the first step in cognitive restructuring. Common cognitive distortions include:

- All-or-Nothing Thinking: Viewing situations in black-and-white terms without recognizing any middle ground. For example, "If I don't succeed perfectly, I'm a complete failure."

- Overgeneralization: Making broad conclusions based on a single event. For example, "I made a mistake in my presentation; I'm always terrible at public speaking."

- Catastrophizing: Expecting the worst possible outcome in any situation. For example, fearing, "If I make a mistake, everyone will think I'm incompetent, and I'll lose my job."

- Mental Filtering: Focusing solely on the negative aspects of a situation while ignoring the positive. For example, dwelling on a minor criticism while disregarding praise.

- Disqualifying the Positive: Rejecting positive experiences by insisting they don't count for some reason. For example, "They only said nice things to be polite, not because I did a good job."

- Jumping to Conclusions: Making negative assumptions without evidence. This includes mind reading (assuming others are thinking negatively about you) and fortune telling (predicting negative outcomes).

- Emotional Reasoning: Assuming that negative emotions reflect the truth. For example, thinking, "I feel anxious, so there must be something wrong."

- Should Statements: Using "should" or "must" statements to impose unrealistic expectations on oneself or others. For example, "I should always be calm and composed."

- Labeling and Mislabeling: Attaching a negative label to oneself or others based on a single incident. For example, calling oneself a "loser" after one setback.

- Personalization: Taking responsibility for events outside of one's control. For example, believing, "It's my fault that the meeting didn't go well."

Cognitive distortions persist because they often operate automatically and are deeply ingrained in our thinking patterns. These distorted thoughts may have been reinforced over time through past experiences, learned behaviors, or emotional conditioning. For instance, if someone has experienced criticism in social situations, they might develop a tendency to overgeneralize, believing they will always be judged negatively by others. The persistence of these distortions can maintain and exacerbate anxiety, as individuals become trapped in a cycle of negative thinking and avoidance.

Cognitive distortions play a significant role in the development and maintenance of anxiety disorders. They can:

- Exacerbate Negative Emotions: Distorted thoughts amplify negative emotions, such as fear, guilt, or sadness, leading to heightened anxiety.

- Reinforce Avoidance Behaviors: When individuals believe their distorted thoughts, they are more likely to engage in avoidance behaviors, which temporarily relieve anxiety but perpetuate it in the long term.

- Undermine Self-Esteem: Persistent cognitive distortions can erode self-esteem and self-worth, making it difficult for individuals to trust their abilities or feel confident in social situations.

- Create a Self-Fulfilling Prophecy: Cognitive distortions can lead to behaviors that inadvertently confirm the negative beliefs, creating a cycle that reinforces the anxiety.

Once cognitive distortions have been identified, the next step is to challenge and reframe them. Several techniques can be used to do this effectively:

- Socratic Questioning
    - Socratic questioning involves asking a series of guided questions to challenge the validity of negative thoughts. This method encourages critical thinking and helps uncover the underlying assumptions behind the thought.
    - Example Questions:
        - What evidence do I have for and against this thought?
        - Is this thought based on facts or assumptions?
        - What's the worst that could happen? How likely is it?
        - How would I advise a friend who had this thought?
        - Is there a more balanced way to look at this situation?

- Cognitive Restructuring Worksheet
    - A cognitive restructuring worksheet is a structured tool that guides individuals through the process of identifying, challenging, and reframing negative thoughts.
    - Exercise:
        - Situation: Describe the situation that triggered the negative thought.
        - Automatic Thought: Identify the negative thought that arose.
        - Emotion: Note the emotion you felt and rate its intensity (0-100%).
        - Evidence For: List the evidence that supports the negative thought.
        - Evidence Against: List the evidence that contradicts the negative thought.
        - Alternative Thought: Develop a more balanced, realistic thought.
        - Outcome: Reflect on how you feel after reframing the thought and rate the intensity of the original emotion again.

- Evidence Collection
    - Evidence collection involves gathering information that contradicts the negative thought, which can weaken its impact and make it easier to reframe.
    - Exercise:
        - Identify the Negative Thought: Write down the thought you want to challenge.
        - Gather Evidence: List specific examples from your past experiences that contradict the negative thought.
        - Develop an Alternative Thought: Based on the evidence, create a more balanced and realistic thought.

- Behavioral Experiments
    - Behavioral experiments involve testing the validity of negative thoughts through real-life experiences. By confronting the feared situation, individuals can gather evidence that disproves their negative beliefs.
    - Exercise:
        - Identify the Negative Thought: Write down the thought you want to test.
        - Design the Experiment: Plan an activity that challenges this thought. For example, if you believe "People will think I'm boring," engage in a social situation and observe the outcome.
        - Conduct the Experiment: Engage in the activity and note what happens.
        - Reflect on the Results: Compare the actual outcome to your predicted outcome. What did you learn?

- Thought Stopping
  - Thought stopping is a technique used to interrupt and redirect negative thought patterns. It is particularly useful for repetitive or intrusive thoughts.
  - Exercise:
    - Recognize the Thought: Become aware of the negative thought as soon as it arises.
    - Stop the Thought: Say "stop" out loud or in your mind. You can also visualize a stop sign.
    - Redirect Your Attention: Immediately focus on a positive or neutral thought or engage in a distracting activity.

For individuals who have mastered the basics of cognitive restructuring, advanced techniques can offer deeper insights and more nuanced approaches to challenging negative thoughts:

- Cognitive Defusion
  - Cognitive defusion, a concept from Acceptance and Commitment Therapy (ACT), involves distancing oneself from thoughts rather than trying to change them. The goal is to see thoughts as mental events, not as truths.
  - Exercise: When a negative thought arises, label it as "just a thought" rather than an absolute reality. For example, instead of saying, "I'm a failure," say, "I'm having the thought that I'm a failure." This creates psychological distance and reduces the thought's emotional impact.

- Downward Arrow Technique
  - This technique involves identifying the core belief underlying a negative thought by asking "What does this thought mean to me?" repeatedly. It helps uncover deeply held beliefs that contribute to anxiety.
  - Exercise: Start with a negative thought, such as "I'm worried about this presentation." Ask yourself, "If this is true, what does it mean?" Continue asking until you reach a core belief, such as "I'm not good enough." This core belief can then be challenged and reframed.

- Double-Standard Technique
  - This technique involves treating oneself with the same compassion and understanding that one would offer to a friend. It helps reduce self-criticism and promotes self-compassion.
  - Exercise: When you notice a self-critical thought, ask yourself, "Would I say this to a friend who was in the same situation?" If the answer is no, reframe the thought with the same kindness and understanding you would offer to someone else.

- Reattribution
  - Reattribution involves identifying external factors that contribute to a situation, rather than attributing it solely to personal failings. This technique is particularly useful for those who tend to personalize events.
  - Exercise: When you find yourself blaming yourself for a negative outcome, list all the factors that contributed to the situation, including external circumstances and the actions of others. This helps create a more balanced perspective.

Case Study: Overcoming Catastrophizing

Consider Sarah, a 32-year-old woman who struggles with anxiety related to her job. Sarah often catastrophizes, believing that if she makes even a small mistake, she will lose her job. Her therapist introduces her to cognitive restructuring:

- Identifying the Cognitive Distortion: Sarah identifies her thought "If I make a mistake, I'll get fired" as catastrophizing.

- Socratic Questioning: Her therapist asks, "What evidence do you have that you'll be fired for a mistake?" Sarah realizes that she has received positive feedback in the past and that her company values her work.

- Alternative Thought: Based on the evidence, Sarah develops a more balanced thought: "Mistakes happen, and I can learn from them. My job performance is generally good, and one mistake won't change that."

- Behavioral Experiment: Sarah decides to test her new thought by taking on a challenging project at work. She notices that even when minor mistakes occur, she receives support and constructive feedback rather than criticism.

- Outcome: Sarah's anxiety decreases, and she feels more confident in her ability to handle challenges at work.

Case Study: Managing Social Anxiety through Cognitive Restructuring

John, a 29-year-old man, experiences significant anxiety in social situations. He often believes that people are judging him harshly and that he will embarrass himself. Through cognitive restructuring, John works on challenging these beliefs:

- Identifying the Cognitive Distortion: John identifies his thoughts "Everyone is judging me" and "I will embarrass myself" as examples of mind reading and catastrophizing.

- Socratic Questioning: John asks himself, "What evidence do I have that people are judging me?" He realizes that he has no concrete evidence to support this belief. He also considers, "What's the worst that could happen if I do embarrass myself?" and concludes that even if he did make a mistake, it likely wouldn't be as disastrous as he fears.

- Alternative Thought: John reframes his thoughts to "Most people are focused on themselves, not on judging me" and "If I make a mistake, it's not the end of the world."

- Behavioral Experiment: John challenges himself to attend a social event and engage in conversations. Afterward, he reflects on the experience and realizes that people were friendly and that no one seemed to judge him harshly.

- **Outcome**: John's social anxiety decreases as he continues to challenge and reframe his thoughts, leading to greater confidence in social situations.

Chapter 8
Managing Relapse and Maintaining Progress

Cognitive-Behavioral Therapy (CBT) provides effective tools for managing anxiety, but like any therapeutic approach, maintaining progress and preventing relapse are critical for long-term success. This chapter focuses on strategies for sustaining the gains made through CBT, recognizing early signs of relapse, and implementing techniques to prevent setbacks. By building resilience and reinforcing positive changes, individuals can continue to manage anxiety effectively over time.

Relapse refers to the return of anxiety symptoms after a period of improvement. It is a common experience for many people and does not signify failure but rather a part of the recovery process. Understanding and preparing for potential relapse is essential for maintaining progress.

Relapse can occur for various reasons, including:

- Stressful Life Events: Significant life changes, such as job loss, relationship issues, or health problems, can trigger a return of anxiety symptoms.

- Lack of Ongoing Practice: Without regular use of CBT techniques, the skills learned in therapy may weaken, making it easier for old patterns of thinking and behavior to resurface.

- Negative Thinking Patterns: Cognitive distortions may re-emerge during challenging times, leading to increased anxiety.

- Avoidance Behaviors: Avoiding anxiety-provoking situations can temporarily reduce discomfort but may reinforce anxiety in the long run, contributing to relapse.

- Overconfidence: Believing that anxiety is completely "cured" may lead some individuals to stop practicing the skills they learned, increasing the risk of relapse.

Early recognition of relapse is crucial for taking action before symptoms fully return. Some early warning signs include:

- Increased Anxiety Levels: Noticing a gradual increase in anxiety, particularly in situations that had been manageable.

- Negative Thought Patterns: Observing a return of cognitive distortions, such as catastrophizing or all-or-nothing thinking.

- Avoidance: Starting to avoid situations or activities that were previously manageable.

- Decreased Use of Coping Strategies: Not practicing relaxation techniques, cognitive restructuring, or other coping skills as regularly as before.

- Physical Symptoms: Experiencing increased physical symptoms of anxiety, such as headaches, stomachaches, or muscle tension.

A relapse prevention plan is a proactive strategy that outlines the steps to take if early signs of relapse are noticed. This plan helps individuals stay on track and reinforces the skills learned in CBT.

- Identify Triggers
  - List specific situations, thoughts, or behaviors that have triggered anxiety or relapse in the past. Being aware of these triggers can help in taking preventive measures.

- Early Warning Signs
  - Identify the personal signs that indicate a possible relapse. This could include changes in mood, behavior, or thinking patterns.

- Action Steps
    - Develop a list of action steps to take if early warning signs appear. These might include revisiting CBT techniques, increasing the use of relaxation exercises, seeking support from a therapist, or engaging in positive activities.

- Support System
    - Identify trusted individuals, such as friends, family members, or a therapist, who can provide support during challenging times. Let them know about your relapse prevention plan so they can assist if needed.

- Self-Compassion
    - Incorporate self-compassion into your plan. Remind yourself that relapse is a normal part of the recovery process and that it's an opportunity to reinforce the skills you've learned.

Maintaining progress after CBT requires ongoing effort and commitment to using the skills learned during therapy. Here are some strategies to help sustain progress:

- Regular Practice of CBT Techniques
    - Cognitive Restructuring: Continue to challenge negative thoughts and replace them with balanced, realistic ones. Regularly use cognitive restructuring worksheets to stay engaged in the process.
    - Behavioral Activation: Keep scheduling and participating in positive activities, especially those that align with your values and goals. This helps maintain a sense of accomplishment and joy.
    - Mindfulness: Integrate mindfulness practices into your daily routine to stay grounded and present. This can help prevent the re-emergence of automatic negative thoughts.

- Lifestyle Changes
    - Healthy Habits: Maintain a healthy lifestyle by eating a balanced diet, getting regular exercise, and prioritizing sleep. These habits support mental well-being and reduce the risk of relapse.
    - Stress Management: Use stress management techniques, such as deep breathing, progressive muscle relaxation, or yoga, to cope with life's challenges effectively.
    - Time Management: Organize your time to balance work, leisure, and self-care activities. Effective time management can prevent burnout and reduce anxiety.

- Social Support
    - Stay Connected: Maintain relationships with supportive friends, family members, or peers who understand your journey and can offer encouragement.
    - Join Support Groups: Consider joining a support group where you can share experiences and gain insights from others who are managing anxiety. This sense of community can be reassuring and motivating.
    - Communicate Needs: Don't hesitate to communicate your needs to those around you, especially during stressful times. Let others know how they can support you in maintaining your progress.

- Continued Therapy
    - Booster Sessions: Schedule occasional "booster" therapy sessions to reinforce the skills learned in CBT and address any new challenges that arise.
    - Therapist Check-Ins: Even after completing CBT, staying in touch with your therapist for periodic check-ins can provide additional support and guidance.

- Reflect and Adjust
    - Regular Reflection: Periodically reflect on your progress, noting what's working well and what might need adjustment. This helps you stay aware of your mental health and make proactive changes when needed.
    - Set New Goals: As you progress, set new, achievable goals that continue to challenge and motivate you. This could involve personal growth, professional development, or exploring new hobbies.
    - Celebrate Successes: Acknowledge and celebrate your successes, no matter how small. Recognizing your achievements reinforces positive behavior and builds confidence.

Resilience is the ability to adapt to challenges and recover from setbacks. Building resilience can help you manage stress, reduce the risk of relapse, and maintain your progress over time.

- Develop a Growth Mindset
    - Embrace Challenges: View challenges as opportunities for growth rather than threats. A growth mindset fosters resilience by encouraging you to learn from difficult experiences.
    - Learn from Setbacks: Instead of seeing setbacks as failures, see them as learning experiences. Reflect on what you can improve and how you can apply this knowledge in the future.

- Strengthen Problem-Solving Skills
    - Proactive Problem-Solving: When faced with a potential relapse trigger, engage in proactive problem-solving. Identify the problem, generate possible solutions, and implement the most effective one.
    - Flexibility in Thinking: Cultivate flexible thinking by considering multiple perspectives and being open to alternative solutions. This reduces the likelihood of rigid, negative thinking patterns that contribute to anxiety.

- Enhance Emotional Regulation
  - Mindfulness for Emotional Awareness: Regular mindfulness practice helps you become more aware of your emotions without being overwhelmed by them. This awareness allows you to respond to emotions in a balanced and thoughtful manner.
  - Emotion Regulation Strategies: Use emotion regulation strategies, such as cognitive restructuring and relaxation techniques, to manage intense emotions before they escalate into anxiety.

- Cultivate a Supportive Environment
  - Positive Relationships: Surround yourself with people who support your well-being and growth. Positive relationships provide emotional support and can buffer against the impact of stress.
  - Healthy Boundaries: Set and maintain healthy boundaries with others to protect your mental health. This might involve saying no to demands that exceed your capacity or distancing yourself from negative influences.

- Practice Gratitude
  - Daily Gratitude Practice: Incorporate a daily gratitude practice into your routine by writing down three things you're grateful for each day. Gratitude fosters a positive mindset and can counterbalance negative thoughts.
  - Gratitude in Relationships: Express gratitude to those who support you. Acknowledging the positive contributions of others strengthens relationships and reinforces your support system.

Case Study: Creating a Relapse Prevention Plan

Consider Jane, a 40-year-old woman who completed CBT for generalized anxiety disorder. Jane experienced significant improvement but wanted to ensure she could maintain her progress and prevent relapse. With her therapist, Jane developed a relapse prevention plan:

- Identify Triggers: Jane identified specific triggers, such as work-related stress and social events where she felt judged, that had contributed to her anxiety in the past.

- Early Warning Signs: Jane noticed that when she started to feel overwhelmed, she would experience increased muscle tension, negative thoughts about her abilities, and a desire to avoid social situations.

- Action Steps: Jane's action steps included revisiting her cognitive restructuring exercises, increasing her practice of mindfulness meditation, and reaching out to her therapist if her anxiety levels began to rise.

- Support System: Jane informed her close friends and family members about her plan and asked them to check in with her regularly. She also scheduled monthly check-ins with her therapist to stay accountable.

- Self-Compassion: Jane included reminders in her plan to practice self-compassion, especially during times of stress. She used positive affirmations to counteract self-criticism and reminded herself that setbacks were part of the recovery process.

Case Study: Maintaining Progress through Mindfulness and
Social Support

Michael, a 45-year-old man, successfully completed CBT for
social anxiety disorder. To maintain his progress, he integrated
mindfulness practices and built a strong social support network:

- Daily Mindfulness Practice: Michael committed to
  practicing mindfulness meditation for 15 minutes every
  morning. This practice helped him stay present and
  manage anxiety-provoking thoughts before they
  escalated.

- Social Support: Michael joined a local support group for
  individuals managing anxiety, where he shared his
  experiences and gained insights from others. The group
  provided him with encouragement and motivation to
  continue practicing the skills he learned in CBT.

- Booster Therapy Sessions: Michael scheduled quarterly
  booster sessions with his therapist to review his progress,
  discuss any challenges, and reinforce his coping strategies.

- Setting New Goals: As Michael's confidence grew, he set
  new goals, such as participating in social events and giving
  presentations at work. Achieving these goals further
  reinforced his progress and reduced his anxiety.

- Reflecting on Successes: Michael kept a journal where he
  reflected on his successes and the strategies that worked
  well for him. This practice boosted his self-esteem and
  helped him stay focused on his growth.

Chapter 9
Building a Long-Term Self-Care Routine

Self-care is the foundation of mental and emotional well-being. Developing a long-term self-care routine is essential for managing anxiety, preventing relapse, and maintaining overall health. This chapter will explore the principles of self-care, offer practical strategies for building a sustainable self-care routine, and provide tools to help individuals integrate self-care into their daily lives.

Self-care involves intentional activities that nurture your physical, emotional, and mental well-being. It is not just about pampering yourself, but about taking proactive steps to maintain balance and resilience in your life. Effective self-care helps you manage stress, reduce anxiety, and enhance your overall quality of life.

The Importance of Self-Care

- Preventing Burnout: Regular self-care helps prevent burnout by reducing stress and replenishing your energy levels.

- Enhancing Resilience: Self-care builds emotional and mental resilience, enabling you to cope with challenges more effectively.

- Supporting Mental Health: Consistent self-care practices can reduce anxiety, depression, and other mental health issues by promoting balance and well-being.

- Improving Physical Health: Physical self-care, such as exercise, nutrition, and sleep, directly impacts your mental health and helps you maintain overall wellness.

- Fostering Self-Compassion: Engaging in self-care is an act of self-compassion, showing that you value yourself and your well-being.

A well-rounded self-care routine addresses various aspects of your life. The core components include:

- Physical Self-Care
    - Exercise: Regular physical activity boosts mood, reduces anxiety, and improves overall health. It can be as simple as walking, yoga, or dancing.
    - Nutrition: Eating a balanced diet rich in nutrients supports brain health and emotional stability. Include a variety of fruits, vegetables, lean proteins, and whole grains.
    - Sleep: Prioritizing sleep is crucial for mental and physical health. Aim for 7-9 hours of quality sleep each night and establish a relaxing bedtime routine.
    - Hydration: Staying hydrated is essential for cognitive function and mood regulation. Aim to drink enough water throughout the day.

- Emotional Self-Care
    - Mindfulness and Meditation: Practicing mindfulness and meditation helps you stay present, reduce stress, and manage anxiety. Even a few minutes of daily practice can make a significant difference.
    - Journaling: Writing down your thoughts and feelings can help you process emotions, gain insights, and reduce mental clutter.
    - Emotional Awareness: Regularly check in with your emotions and acknowledge them without judgment. This practice helps you stay connected to your emotional state and respond more effectively.

- Mental Self-Care
    - Cognitive Restructuring: Continue to challenge negative thoughts and replace them with balanced, realistic ones. This practice is key to maintaining a healthy mindset.
    - Learning and Growth: Engage in activities that stimulate your mind and promote personal growth, such as reading, taking a course, or learning a new skill.
    - Creative Expression: Engage in creative activities, such as painting, writing, or playing music, to express yourself and relieve stress.

- Social Self-Care
  - Connecting with Others: Maintain meaningful relationships with friends, family, and peers. Regular social interaction is important for emotional support and a sense of belonging.
  - Setting Boundaries: Establish and maintain healthy boundaries in relationships to protect your well-being. This might involve saying no to demands that exceed your capacity or distancing yourself from toxic influences.
  - Support Systems: Identify and nurture your support systems, whether they include friends, family, a therapist, or a support group.

- Spiritual Self-Care
  - Mindfulness and Meditation: Engage in practices that connect you to your inner self and promote a sense of peace and purpose.
  - Nature: Spending time in nature can be a spiritual experience that refreshes your mind and spirit. Activities like hiking, gardening, or simply sitting in a park can be deeply restorative.
  - Reflection: Regularly reflect on your values, beliefs, and what gives your life meaning. This reflection can guide your actions and help you live in alignment with your true self.

Creating a sustainable self-care routine involves identifying practices that resonate with you and can be consistently integrated into your life. Here's how to build a routine that works:

- Start Small
  - Begin with small, manageable self-care activities that you can easily incorporate into your daily routine. For example, start with 5 minutes of mindfulness practice or a short walk each day.
  - Realistic Expectations: Understand that self-care doesn't have to be time-consuming. Small, consistent efforts can be more effective than sporadic, intensive activities. Starting small helps build a habit that feels manageable and sustainable.

- Prioritize Consistency
    - Consistency is more important than intensity. Focus on making self-care a regular part of your routine rather than trying to do too much at once. Small, consistent practices lead to lasting change.
    - Daily Rituals: Establish daily rituals, such as a morning meditation or evening gratitude journaling, that become ingrained in your routine. These rituals anchor your day and provide a consistent touchpoint for self-care.

- Tailor to Your Needs
    - Customize your self-care routine to fit your individual needs, preferences, and lifestyle. Choose activities that you enjoy and that bring you a sense of fulfillment.
    - Personalized Self-Care: Recognize that self-care is not one-size-fits-all. What works for someone else may not work for you. Tailor your routine to your unique needs and preferences, whether that means more physical activity, creative expression, or quiet reflection.

- Set Realistic Goals
    - Set achievable goals for your self-care practices. For example, aim to exercise three times a week or journal for 10 minutes each morning. Gradually increase your goals as you build momentum.
    - SMART Goals: Use the SMART framework (Specific, Measurable, Achievable, Relevant, Time-bound) to set clear and realistic self-care goals. For example, "I will meditate for 5 minutes every morning for the next two weeks."

- Schedule Self-Care
    - Treat self-care as an essential part of your schedule. Block out time in your calendar for self-care activities, just as you would for work or other commitments.
    - Time Management: Incorporate self-care into your daily schedule by blocking specific times for activities, whether it's a 10-minute morning stretch or a weekly hour-long hobby. Prioritizing self-care in your calendar ensures it becomes a non-negotiable part of your routine.

- Be Flexible
    - Allow for flexibility in your self-care routine. Life can be unpredictable, so it's important to adapt your practices as needed. If you miss a day, don't be hard on yourself —just get back on track the next day.
    - Adapting to Life's Demands: Recognize that life can be unpredictable, and sometimes self-care may need to be adjusted. Flexibility in your routine allows you to adapt to changing circumstances without feeling guilty or overwhelmed.

- Incorporate Variety
    - Include a variety of self-care activities in your routine to address different aspects of your well-being. This variety keeps your routine interesting and ensures a holistic approach to self-care.
    - Balanced Self-Care: Incorporate activities that address physical, emotional, mental, and spiritual well-being. For example, balance exercise with meditation, social time with quiet reflection, and work with play.

- Reflect and Adjust
    - Regularly reflect on your self-care routine to see what's working and what might need adjustment. Be open to trying new activities and making changes to better meet your needs.
    - Regular Check-Ins: Set aside time each month to review your self-care routine. Reflect on what's working, what's not, and how you feel overall. Use this time to adjust your routine as needed.

Self-care doesn't have to be time-consuming or complicated. Many self-care practices can be seamlessly integrated into your daily life:

- Mindful Morning Routine
    - Start your day with a mindful morning routine that sets a positive tone. This might include deep breathing, stretching, a healthy breakfast, and setting intentions for the day.
    - Intentional Start: Waking up 10-15 minutes earlier to engage in a mindful activity can set a calm and positive tone for the day. Use this time for a quick meditation, journaling, or gentle stretching.

- Lunch Break Relaxation
    - Use your lunch break to recharge by taking a short walk, practicing mindfulness, or enjoying a healthy meal. This break helps reduce stress and boosts afternoon productivity.
    - Midday Reset: Incorporate a brief relaxation exercise during lunch, such as a 5-minute deep breathing session or a short walk outside. This helps you reset and approach the rest of the day with renewed energy.

- Evening Wind-Down
    - Create an evening routine that helps you unwind and prepare for restful sleep. This might include reading, gentle yoga, or listening to calming music.
    - Transition to Sleep: Establish a calming pre-sleep routine that might include dimming the lights, sipping herbal tea, or practicing relaxation techniques. These activities signal your body that it's time to wind down and prepare for rest.

- Incorporating Movement
    - Find ways to incorporate movement into your day, such as taking the stairs, stretching at your desk, or doing a quick workout. Regular movement supports both physical and mental health.
    - Active Breaks: Set reminders to take short breaks for stretching or a quick walk, especially if you have a sedentary job. Regular movement throughout the day helps maintain energy levels and reduces tension.

- Mindful Eating
    - Practice mindful eating by paying attention to the taste, texture, and aroma of your food. This practice enhances your enjoyment of meals and helps you make healthier food choices.
    - Present-Moment Awareness: Focus on the sensory experience of eating, such as the taste, texture, and smell of your food. This practice not only enhances enjoyment but also promotes healthier eating habits by preventing overeating.

- Gratitude Practice
    - End your day with a gratitude practice by reflecting on three things you're grateful for. This practice shifts your focus to positive aspects of your life and promotes a sense of well-being.
    - Positive Reflection: Keep a journal by your bedside and write down three things you're grateful for each night. Reflecting on positive experiences can enhance your mood and help you approach life with a more positive outlook.

Despite its importance, self-care can be challenging to maintain due to various barriers. Here's how to overcome common obstacles:

- Lack of Time
    - Solution: Start with short, simple self-care activities that can be easily integrated into your day. For example, take 5 minutes to practice deep breathing or do a quick stretch.
    - Time Audit: Conduct a time audit to identify pockets of time that can be used for self-care. You might find that you can repurpose time spent on less fulfilling activities.

- Guilt
  - Solution: Reframe self-care as a necessary investment in your well-being rather than an indulgence. Remember that taking care of yourself enables you to be more present and effective in other areas of your life.
  - Positive Affirmations: Use positive affirmations to combat feelings of guilt, such as "I deserve to take care of myself" or "Self-care is essential for my well-being."

- Inconsistent Motivation
  - Solution: Set small, achievable goals that build momentum and create a sense of accomplishment. Celebrate your successes to reinforce positive behavior.
  - Accountability: Consider enlisting a friend or family member to join you in self-care activities. Having a self-care partner can boost motivation and make the experience more enjoyable.

- Unrealistic Expectations
  - Solution: Set realistic expectations for your self-care routine. It's okay if your routine isn't perfect or if you miss a day. Focus on consistency and progress rather than perfection.
  - Self-Compassion: Practice self-compassion by being gentle with yourself when things don't go as planned. Remind yourself that self-care is a journey, not a destination.

- External Pressure
  - Solution: Set boundaries with others to protect your self-care time. Communicate your needs clearly and assertively, and prioritize your well-being even when external pressures arise.
  - Boundary Setting: Practice saying no to demands that conflict with your self-care routine. This might involve declining invitations or delegating tasks to others.

As you become more comfortable with your self-care routine, consider enhancing it by exploring new practices, deepening your current practices, or expanding the areas of self-care you focus on.

- Exploring New Practices
    - Try New Activities: Experiment with different self-care activities to see what resonates with you. This might include exploring new forms of exercise, trying out different mindfulness techniques, or engaging in a creative hobby.
    - Community Engagement: Consider joining a group or community focused on a shared interest, such as a yoga class, book club, or volunteer organization. Engaging with others who share your interests can enrich your self-care routine.

- Deepening Current Practices
    - Mindfulness and Meditation: If you're already practicing mindfulness or meditation, consider deepening your practice by increasing the duration, exploring new techniques, or attending a retreat.
    - Creative Expression: If you enjoy creative activities, challenge yourself to explore new forms of expression, such as trying a new art medium, writing genre, or musical instrument.

- Expanding Your Focus
    - Holistic Approach: Ensure your self-care routine addresses all aspects of your well-being, including physical, emotional, mental, social, and spiritual needs. Expanding your focus can lead to a more balanced and fulfilling self-care routine.
    - Life Balance: Consider how your self-care routine supports a balanced life. This might involve ensuring that you're not neglecting one area of life, such as relationships or career, in favor of another.

Case Study: Developing a Long-Term Self-Care Routine

Emma, a 35-year-old woman, struggled with anxiety and burnout due to a demanding job and family responsibilities. After completing CBT, she recognized the importance of self-care in maintaining her progress and preventing relapse. Emma worked with her therapist to develop a long-term self-care routine:

- Physical Self-Care: Emma committed to a 30-minute daily walk and started incorporating more fruits and vegetables into her diet. She also established a consistent sleep schedule.

- Emotional Self-Care: Emma began journaling every evening to process her emotions and reflect on her day. She also practiced mindfulness meditation for 10 minutes each morning.

- Mental Self-Care: Emma set aside time each week to read books on personal development and engage in creative writing, which she found to be a relaxing and fulfilling outlet.

- Social Self-Care: Emma made a point to schedule regular coffee dates with friends and joined a local book club to expand her social network.

- Spiritual Self-Care: Emma started spending time in nature every weekend, hiking or gardening, which she found to be spiritually rejuvenating. She also practiced gratitude by reflecting on what she was thankful for each day.

Case Study: Overcoming Barriers to Self-Care

James, a 40-year-old father of two, found it difficult to maintain a self-care routine due to work pressures and family responsibilities. He felt guilty taking time for himself and often neglected his own needs. With the help of a therapist, James developed strategies to overcome these barriers:

- Lack of Time: James started by incorporating small self-care practices into his daily routine, such as stretching for 5 minutes in the morning and taking short walks during his lunch break. He also conducted a time audit to identify where he could make more time for self-care.

- Guilt: James reframed self-care as a necessary investment in his well-being, which would allow him to be a better partner, father, and employee. He used positive affirmations to combat feelings of guilt, such as "Taking care of myself helps me take care of others."

- Inconsistent Motivation: James set small, achievable goals for his self-care routine and enlisted his wife as an accountability partner. They both agreed to support each other's self-care efforts and made it a priority in their household.

- External Pressure: James practiced setting boundaries with his employer and family members to protect his self-care time. He learned to say no to additional work demands that conflicted with his self-care routine and delegated some household tasks to other family members.

Chapter 10
Personal Growth and Future Goals

Overcoming anxiety is a significant achievement, but it's also a stepping stone toward greater personal growth. This chapter explores how to continue evolving by setting and achieving future goals and embracing new challenges. The journey of personal growth is ongoing, and by setting meaningful goals, you can continue to build on the progress you've made and thrive in all areas of your life.

Personal growth involves the ongoing process of developing yourself, both personally and professionally. It's about striving to become the best version of yourself by learning, evolving, and expanding your potential. This growth is essential for maintaining well-being, achieving fulfillment, and living a purposeful life.

The Role of Personal Growth in Maintaining Mental Health

- Continued Self-Improvement: Engaging in personal growth activities helps prevent stagnation and keeps you motivated. The pursuit of growth fosters a sense of purpose and direction.

- Building Resilience: Personal growth challenges you to step outside your comfort zone, which builds resilience and enhances your ability to cope with future challenges.

- Enhancing Self-Esteem: Achieving personal goals and learning new skills boost self-esteem and confidence. This reinforces positive self-concepts and promotes mental well-being.

- Preventing Relapse: By focusing on personal growth, you stay engaged in positive activities that keep your mind active and prevent a relapse into old patterns of anxiety.

Goal-setting is a powerful tool for personal growth. When you set and achieve goals, you create a sense of accomplishment and direction in your life. Here's how to set meaningful goals that align with your values and aspirations:

- Identify Your Core Values
  - Reflect on What Matters Most: Identify your core values—those principles and beliefs that guide your life. These might include family, health, creativity, integrity, or community.
  - Align Goals with Values: Set goals that reflect your core values. When your goals align with what truly matters to you, you're more likely to stay motivated and committed.

- Use the SMART Framework
  - Specific: Define your goal clearly. What exactly do you want to achieve?
  - Measurable: Determine how you'll measure your progress. What indicators will tell you that you're on the right track?
  - Achievable: Ensure your goal is realistic and attainable given your current resources and constraints.
  - Relevant: Make sure your goal is meaningful and relevant to your life and long-term objectives.
  - Time-Bound: Set a deadline for your goal. When do you want to achieve it?

- Break Goals into Smaller Steps
  - Create a Step-by-Step Plan: Break down your larger goal into smaller, manageable tasks. This makes the goal less overwhelming and allows you to make steady progress.
  - Set Milestones: Establish milestones or checkpoints along the way. These mini-goals help you track progress and stay motivated.

- Stay Flexible
    - Adapt to Changes: Life is unpredictable, and sometimes your goals may need to change. Stay flexible and be willing to adjust your goals as circumstances evolve.
    - Reevaluate Regularly: Periodically review your goals to ensure they still align with your values and aspirations. Adjust them as needed to stay on track.

Personal growth can occur in various areas of your life. Here are some key areas to consider:

- Career Growth
    - Skills Development: Focus on acquiring new skills or enhancing existing ones. This might include taking courses, attending workshops, or seeking mentorship.
    - Professional Networking: Build and maintain professional relationships that can support your career growth. Networking can lead to new opportunities and collaborations.
    - Setting Career Goals: Define where you want to go in your career and set specific goals to get there. This might include aiming for a promotion, changing careers, or starting your own business.

- Educational Growth
    - Lifelong Learning: Embrace the mindset of lifelong learning. This could involve pursuing formal education, such as a degree or certification, or engaging in self-study through books, online courses, and seminars.
    - Expanding Knowledge: Focus on expanding your knowledge in areas that interest you. This could be related to your career, hobbies, or personal development.

- Emotional Growth
  - Emotional Intelligence: Work on developing emotional intelligence by improving your ability to recognize, understand, and manage your own emotions, as well as empathize with others.
  - Self-Reflection: Regularly engage in self-reflection to understand your emotions, thoughts, and behaviors. This can lead to greater self-awareness and emotional maturity.

- Physical Growth
  - Health and Fitness: Set goals related to improving your physical health, such as exercising regularly, eating a balanced diet, or getting enough sleep.
  - Physical Challenges: Consider taking on physical challenges, such as running a marathon, learning a new sport, or practicing yoga. These challenges can boost your physical and mental resilience.

- Spiritual Growth
  - Mindfulness and Meditation: Continue to deepen your mindfulness and meditation practices as part of your spiritual growth. These practices can help you connect with your inner self and find peace.
  - Exploring Spirituality: If spirituality is important to you, explore practices and beliefs that resonate with you. This might include studying religious texts, engaging in prayer, or participating in spiritual communities.

- Social Growth
  - Building Relationships: Focus on building and maintaining healthy relationships with friends, family, and colleagues. Strong relationships contribute to emotional well-being and personal fulfillment.
  - Community Involvement: Get involved in your community by volunteering, joining local groups, or participating in social causes. This not only helps others but also fosters a sense of belonging and purpose.

Growth is most effective when you regularly reflect on your experiences and seek feedback from others. This ongoing process of self-assessment helps you identify strengths, areas for improvement, and opportunities for further development.

- Regular Reflection
    - Self-Assessment: Make it a habit to regularly assess your progress. Ask yourself what you've learned, how you've grown, and where you can improve.
    - Journaling: Keep a journal where you reflect on your personal growth journey. Document your successes, challenges, and insights. This practice enhances self-awareness and helps you track your progress over time.

- Seeking Feedback
    - Constructive Criticism: Invite constructive feedback from trusted friends, family, or mentors. They can offer valuable perspectives and help you see areas for growth that you might overlook.
    - Peer Feedback: Engage in peer feedback opportunities, such as group projects or community involvement, where you can give and receive feedback in a supportive environment.

- Learning from Mistakes
    - Growth Mindset: Embrace a growth mindset by viewing mistakes as opportunities for learning rather than failures. This mindset encourages continuous improvement and resilience.
    - Analyzing Setbacks: When you experience setbacks, take time to analyze what went wrong and how you can approach similar situations differently in the future. This reflection turns challenges into valuable learning experiences.

- Continuous Learning
    - Staying Curious: Cultivate a mindset of curiosity and openness to new experiences. Lifelong learning keeps your mind active and engaged, promoting continuous personal and professional growth.
    - Diverse Learning Sources: Seek out diverse learning sources, such as books, podcasts, workshops, and online courses, to gain new perspectives and knowledge.

Personal growth is rewarding but can also be challenging. Here are some common obstacles and strategies to overcome them:

- Fear of Failure
    - Reframe Failure as Learning: Instead of viewing failure as a setback, see it as a learning opportunity. Every failure teaches you something valuable that can help you grow.
    - Take Calculated Risks: Personal growth often requires stepping outside your comfort zone. Embrace calculated risks, knowing that growth comes from facing challenges.

- Lack of Motivation
    - Find Your "Why": Connect your goals to your core values and personal aspirations. Understanding why your goals matter to you can boost motivation.
    - Celebrate Small Wins: Recognize and celebrate small achievements along the way. This creates a sense of progress and keeps you motivated.

- Imposter Syndrome
    - Acknowledge Your Achievements: Remind yourself of your successes and the hard work that got you there. You deserve your achievements.
    - Seek Support: Talk to a mentor, coach, or therapist about your feelings of self-doubt. They can offer perspective and help you build confidence.

- Procrastination
    - Break Tasks into Smaller Steps: Procrastination often occurs when tasks feel overwhelming. Break your goals into smaller, manageable steps to make them more approachable.
    - Use Time Management Techniques: Techniques like the Pomodoro Technique (working in short bursts with breaks) can help you stay focused and make progress without getting overwhelmed.

- Balancing Growth with Self-Care
    - Avoid Burnout: While pursuing personal growth, it's important to balance ambition with self-care. Ensure you're taking time to rest, relax, and recharge.
    - Set Boundaries: Protect your time and energy by setting boundaries with yourself and others. This helps you stay focused on your goals without overcommitting.

Sustaining momentum in your personal growth journey requires ongoing commitment, adaptability, and a willingness to embrace change.

- Revisiting Goals
    - Regular Review: Set aside time to regularly review your goals. Reflect on your progress, adjust your strategies, and set new goals as needed to stay aligned with your evolving aspirations.
    - Adjusting as Needed: Life circumstances can change, and your goals may need to be adjusted accordingly. Stay flexible and be willing to modify your goals to better fit your current situation.

- Building a Support Network
    - Accountability Partners: Find an accountability partner who shares similar goals or interests. Regular check-ins can help you stay on track and provide mutual support.
    - Mentorship: Seek out mentors who can guide you on your growth journey. A mentor can offer valuable insights, feedback, and encouragement.

- Embracing Change
    - Adaptability: Embrace change as a natural part of life and personal growth. Being adaptable allows you to navigate challenges more effectively and seize new opportunities.
    - Openness to New Experiences: Be open to trying new things and stepping outside your comfort zone. New experiences can lead to unexpected growth and development.

- Celebrating Achievements
    - Recognizing Progress: Take time to acknowledge and celebrate your achievements, both big and small. Celebrating success reinforces positive behavior and motivates continued effort.
    - Sharing Success: Share your achievements with others, whether through social media, a blog, or in conversation with friends and family. Sharing success can inspire others and create a sense of community.

Case Study: Setting and Achieving Future Goals

Samantha, a 30-year-old professional, overcame anxiety through CBT and wanted to focus on personal growth and career advancement. She decided to set specific goals to further her development:

- Career Growth: Samantha identified her desire to move into a leadership role within her company. She set a goal to earn a relevant certification and network with mentors in her field.

- Educational Growth: Samantha enrolled in a part-time online course to enhance her knowledge in leadership and management. She set milestones for completing each module.

- Emotional Growth: To continue her emotional growth, Samantha committed to journaling daily and practicing mindfulness meditation. She also attended workshops on emotional intelligence.

- **Physical Growth:** Samantha set a goal to run a half-marathon within the next year. She created a training plan and joined a local running group for support and accountability.

- **Social Growth:** Samantha aimed to strengthen her relationships by scheduling regular get-togethers with friends and participating in community events. She also volunteered at a local charity.